Natural HEALTH

Peter Benjamin Lebuhn, P.H.D.

Trafford
PUBLISHING   www.trafford.com
North America & international
toll-free: 844-688-6899 (USA & Canada)
fax: 812 355 4082

CONTENTS

CONTENTS

CHAPTER I

Origin Of Holistic Medicine and the uses of Complimentary Medicine in Present Day Healthcare

Written by:

PETER BENJAMIN LEBUHN

Goodwin College of Professional Studies

Course: Foundations of Holistic Medicine
Professor: Sister Rose Scalone

Origin of Holistic Medicine and the uses of Complimentary Medicine in Present Day Healthcare:

A. ORIGIN OF HOLISTIC MEDICINE

Holistic Medicine is an alternative medicine, a form of complimentary and integrative medicine that focuses on personal accountability for one's health, the human body's ability to heal one itself and balancing the body, mind and spirit with the environment. Holistic medicine encompasses acupuncture, biofeedback, faith healing, folk medicine, meditation, megavitamin therapy, yoga and many more. Holistic medicine has its roots in several ancient healing traditions that stress healthy living and being in harmony with nature. Socrates promoted a holistic approach. Plato was another advocate of holism, advising physicians to respect the relationship between mind and body. Hippocrates emphasized the body's ability to heal itself and cautioned physicians not to interfere with this process. It was not until 1926, however, that Jan Christian Smuts coined the term "holism", which has given us the more integrated concept of psychosomatic medicine now known as holistic medicine. In the 1970s, "holistic" became a more common term. Today, holistic medicine is known as an approach to life and health which brings together the physical, mental, and spiritual aspects of a person in order to create a total sense of well being. (See "Holistic Medicine". American Cancer Society) European History throughout Western European history there were two major trends: the professionalism of physicians who belonged to the upper classes and the folk healers who lived among the common people. The professionals developed in order to enhance their status in life, while the folk healers developed out of the necessity to survive. Herbalism and the water cure, hydrotherapy, or naturopathy developed slowly 2,000 years of history. Autocratic traditions developed over time that gave today's European physicians social status and acceptance. During the Greco-Roman Period, interest in the hydrotherapy can be traced back to the ancient Roman spas and the hot mineral springs at Bath, England. During the Dark Ages in Europe, the Catholic church played a central role. At first, the Church suppressed all development. Later on, the Church supported the development of professional physicians. Eventually, the power of the Church literally exterminated much of the competition from folk healers during the witch-hunting period, which spanned more than four centuries (from the 14th to 17th century). Healers throughout the medieval period could come in many varieties. Physicians, who studied the works of the Greek masters at universities, were the elite of the medical profession in the Middle Ages. However few people other than the well off or the nobility had regular access to these. Folk healers passed on their knowledge from master to apprentice, and were more accessible to the common person or laborer than to the physicians. Unregulated, but knowledgeable on herbs and folk-remedies, they were gradually excluded from the medical system. Monastic medicine monasteries played a big part in the provision of medieval medicine. Virtually every monastery had an infirmary for the monks or nuns, and this led to provision being made for the care of secular patients. In the 19th century, a medical reform movement was started in Europe as a reaction against heroic medicine. Germany became the world center of medical research, training, and pharmaceuticals drawing students from all over the world by the world by the end 19th century. Hygiene and public health became the central focus of emerging urbanization. The Western healing practices developed differently in the New World than they did in the Old World. In Europe, physicians already had a centuries old monopoly over the right to treat patients. In America, medical practice was literally open to anyone who called themselves a physician. In America, the popular health movement played a central role in the development of alternative therapy practices. Herbalism, homeopathy, eclecticism and Natural Hygiene developed during the Health Reform Movement. Only homeopathy, natural hygiene and eclecticism managed to last from the 1830s through the rest of the 19th century. During 1890-1920, which is the Progressive era of Health Care Reform, Osteopathy, chiropractic, and naturopathy developed at the turn of the century and up to the present, alternative medicines are still being widely used. (See "Alternative Medicine". Wikipedia, the Free Encyclopedia)

A. BIO-ENERGY HEALING

Reiki

Reiki is a Japanese technique for stress reduction and relaxation that also promotes healing. It is administered by lying on of hands and is based on the premise that an unseen universal energy flows through the body, which is what keeps the human body alive. If one's life force energy is low, then we are more likely to become ill or feel stress, and if our life force is high, we are more capable of being happy and healthy. The word Reiki is made up of two Japanese words –Rei, which means "God's Wisdom or the Higher Power", and Ki, which is "life force energy". We can see that Reiki is actually "spiritually guided life force energy." A treatment feels like a wonderful glowing radiance that flows through and around the client. Reiki treats the whole person including body; emotions, mind and spirit creating many beneficial effects that include relaxation and feelings of peace, security and well being. Many have reported miraculous results.

(See "Reiki". Skeptics Dictionary)

Qi Gong

A component of traditional Chinese medicine that combines movement, meditation, and regulation of breathing to enhance the flow of Qi which is an ancient term given to what is believed to be vital energy in the body, improve blood circulation, and enhance immune function. (See "Qigong, the Ancient Art of Health". About China Online)

How are Reiki and Qi Gong used in healthcare Modalities?

Reiki is a treatment feels like a wonderful glowing radiance that flows through and around you. Reiki treats the whole person including body, emotions, mind and spirit creating many beneficial effects that include relaxation and feelings of peace, security and well being. Many have reported miraculous results. Reiki is a simple, natural and safe method of spiritual healing and self-improvement that everyone can use. It has been effective in helping virtually every known illness and malady and always creates a beneficial effect. It also works in conjunction with all other medical or therapeutic techniques to relieve side effects and promote recovery. An amazingly simple technique to learn, the ability to use Reiki is not taught in the usual sense but is transferred to the student during a Reiki class. This ability is passed on during an "attunement" given by a Reiki master and allows the student to tap into an unlimited supply of "life force energy" to improve one's health and enhance the quality of life. Its use is not dependent on one's intellectual capacity or spiritual development and therefore is available to everyone. It has been successfully taught to thousands of people of all ages and backgrounds. While Reiki is spiritual in nature, it is not a religion. It has no dogma, and there is nothing you must believe in order to learn and use Reiki. In fact, Reiki is not dependent on belief at all and will work whether you believe in the power of Reiki or not. Reiki comes from God, many people find that using Reiki puts them more in touch with the experience of their religion rather than having only an intellectual concept of it. Qi Gong on the other hand, is widely used by millions of people in China and around the world regularly practice qigong as a health maintenance exercise. Qigong and related disciplines are still associated with the martial arts and meditation routines trained by Taoist and Buddhist monks, professional martial artists and their students. Formerly much more closely guarded, in the modern era such practices have become widely available to the general public both in China and around the world. Medical qigong treatment has been officially recognized as a standard medical technique in Chinese hospitals since 1989. It has been included in the curriculum of major universities in China. After years of debate, the Chinese government decided to officially manage qigong through government regulation in 1996 and has also listed qigong as part of their National Health Plan. Qigong can help practitioners to learn Diaphragmatic breathing, an important component of the relaxation response, which is important in combating stress. (See "Reiki and Qigong". Dreamweaver Lodge)

Herbal Treatments

Herbal treatments are using herbs as a medication to particular ailments. This treatment is also known as Herbalism and Herbal medicine and phytotherapy. Herbalism is a folk and traditional medicinal practice based on the use of plant extracts. All plants produce chemical compounds as part of their normal metabolic activities. These can be split into primary metabolites, such as sugars and fats, found in all plants, and secondary metabolites found in a smaller range of plants, some only in a particular genus or species.

The autologous functions of secondary metabolites are varied. For example, as toxins to deter predation, or to attract insects for pollination. It is these secondary metabolites which can have therapeutic actions in humans and which can be refined to produce drugs.

Some examples are insulin from the roots of dahlias, quinine from the cinchona, morphine and codeine from the poppy, and digoxin from the foxglove. Medicinal plants can be used by anyone, for example as part of a salad, an herbal tea or supplement, although some herbs considered dangerous are restricted from sale to the public. Specialist companies may provide such herbs to professional herbalists. Many herbalists, both professional and amateur, often grow or wildcraft their own herbs. Many common weeds have medicinal properties. Medicinal herbs can be used in various forms such as Herbal Teas, Herbal Tinctures, Fluid extracts, Solid Extracts, Herbal Poultices, Powdered Herbs and Tablets, Herbal Creams and Ointments and Essential Oils. (See Herbalism. Wikipedia, the Free Encyclopedia.)

Ayurvedic Medicine

Ayurveda, considered the most ancient existing medical system, is a 4,000 year-old Indian method of healing that includes diet, natural therapies and herbs dependent on body type. Ayurvedic medicine places equal emphasis on body, mind, and spirit. Ayurveda strives to restore the innate harmony of the individual. Ayurveda is a Sanskrit word that means "the science of lifespan." The word ayurveda is made up of two root words: Ayur defined as life and Veda defined as knowledge. According to ayurveda, every human being was created by the cosmos as either male energy, Purusha, or female energy, Prakruti. Purusha is a choiceless passive awareness, while Prakuti is a choiceful active consciousness. A person's self-identify, called Ahamkara, is affected by three universal qualities: satva, rajas, and tamas. Satva equips an individual with the ability to have clarity of perception. Conversely, tamas is responsible for periods of confusion and deep sleep, as well as the tendency towards inertia and darkness. Rajas cause movement, sensations, feelings and emotions, everything that makes us human beings. (See "Ayurvedic Medicine Alternative Medicine Therapies")

Kinesiology

Kinesiology is a brand new branch of science, which was developed by physicians, chiropractors and acupuncturists in America. These physicians used their collective knowledge and integrated western thought to Chinese medicine to develop a totally new technology which is amazingly efficient at balancing the body so that optimum health, energy and strength will be returned. Kinesiology stands apart from any other type of health technology largely due to the use of revolutionary muscle testing. Kinesiology is a truly holistic system, because it looks at the whole individual not just selected parts. When you step on a cat's tail, it's the other end that screams. Kinesiology studies all types of stressors that may cause disease. These stressors include emotional, nutritional, structural and electrical stress. The basis of Kinesiology is that the body is like an electrical piece of equipment, which is controlled by an incredibly complex computer, the brain. The brain is continually in communication with each of the 639 muscles in the body. (See "What is Kinesiology?" Kinesiologist Us)

Studies that Show Actual Healing and Transformation in the lives of patients or clients

Advocates of alternative medicine hold that alternative therapies often provide the public with services that may not be available from western medicine. This argument covers a range of areas, such as patient empowerment, alternative methods of pain management, treatment methods that support the biopsychosocial model of health, stress reduction services, other preventive health services that are not typically a part of western medicine, and of course complementary medicine's palliative care which is practiced by such world renowned cancer centers such as Memorial Sloan-Kettering. Advocates of alternative medicine hold that the various alternative treatment methods are effective in treating a wide range of major and minor medical conditions, and contend that recently published research proves the effectiveness of specific alternative treatments. They assert that a PubMed search revealed over 370,000 research papers classified as alternative medicine published in Medline-recognized journals since 1966 in the National Library of Medicine database advocates of alternative medicine hold that alternative medicine provides health benefits through patient empowerment, by offering more choices to the public, including treatments that are simply not available in western medicine. Some health professionals suggest that cancer pain and side effects of treatment can be managed by using different aspects of holistic medicine that include the physical, psychological, and spiritual factors involved with each person. Increasingly, the health care team is playing an important role in the treatment provided by many research centers and hospitals. Members of this team are drawn from the specialties of medicine, nursing, surgery, radiation therapy, oncology, psychiatry, psychology, and social work. In addition, the team may call on dietitians, physical therapists, and the clergy for support. Health professionals realize that a person's health depends on the balance of physical, psychological, social, and cultural forces. (See Holistic Medicine". American Cancer Society)

REFERENCES

1. "Alternative Medicine". Wikipedia, the Free Encyclopedia. Nov. 2, 2006
   http://en.wikipedia.org/wiki/Alternative_medicine

2. "ReiKi and QiGong ". Dreamweaver Lodge.
   http://www.dreamweaverlodge.com/reikiandqigong.html

3. "What is Kinesiology?" Kinesiologist Us
   http://www.kinesiologist.us/what_is_kinesiology.html

4. "Reiki" The Skeptics Dictionary http://skeptic.com/reiki.html

5. Ayurveda Medicine". Alternative Medicine Therapies
   http://library.thinkquest.org/24206/ayurveda-medicine.html

6. "Herbal Treatments". Wikipedia, the Free Encyclopedia. Nov. 1, 2006

7. "What is Reiki" The International Center for Reiki Training
   http://www.reiki.org/FAQ/WhatIsReiki.html

CHAPTER II

Advanced Reiki Techniques

Written By

PETER BENJAMIN LEBUHN

Professor McClintock

Advanced Reiki Techniques

INTRODUCTION

What is Reiki? It is a Japanese word: universal (rei) life force energy (ki) and Westerners adopted this meaning and their translation of Reiki is "Universal Life Force Energy," (Honervogt, T 1998) The objective of Reiki is stated as "that it works in tandem with your body/mind to bring balance and harmony to your being." (Rebecca Dobnus)

How did Reiki originate? The justification of Reiki is rooted in 1970s discovery of the existence of human energy system that made people believe that human beings are moving energy fields that react with other creatures. This discovery excited the Western world, which then attempted the use of bioenergy for healing. In the USA the works of Dr Thelma Moss who confirmed through her researches that hands send energy to other hands and thus effect healing resembled this. On the other hand in Russia the Kilirian photographing method was used. (Pat Cougar)

Since then further researches on alternative medicine were conducted and professional bodies were established for the purpose and in 1994 a report by the title "Alternative Medicine: Expanding Medical Horizons" was available for everybody. Then eventually in 1995 a Reiki training Centre was established and researches on Reiki were published on a website. (William Rand) Later effect of Reiki on chronic illnesses was studied and patients receiving Reiki healing reported positive results (Letorre, 2005).

HOW REIKI HEALING WORKS

By providing relaxation and reduction of stress Reiki contributes to effecting harmony and balance to the body. In its basic form energy flows from the practitioner's hand on to the recipient. Moreover Reiki has the effect of healing that is different to the traditional curing of symptoms. The healing in Reiki restores the greater wholeness and well-being. "It strives to restore us to our ideal "balance", emotionally, physically and spiritually, thus enabling us to be the highest and truest expression of who we really are." Reiki is described and defined in a number of versions by the practitioner, yet I find the following quote from 'The Use of Reiki in Psychotherapy' by Mary Ann Latorre a precise one:

> "*Reiki works to rebalance the vibrational field within mind and body although there is no agreed-upon theory on how it works or basic understanding for the mechanism of its action. Scientists, however, are beginning to explore the potential role that bioelectromagnetic fields have on physiological processes, making a connection that may eventually provide some theoretical underpinnings for Reiki and other touch therapies (Walleczek, 1995, as cited in Latorre, 2005).*"

It is also claimed that Keiki effects healing by achieving the flow of ki energy through the affected parts of the body, which while flowing breaks apart the blockages and negative energy. This then clears the energy pathways and allows a natural healthy flow of life force.

Despite the fact Reiki originated in the east, today the scientists and doctors of the west are aware of its favourable results and are experimenting the effect of Reiki in inducing healing through the boosting of the immune system.

ADVANCED REIKI TECHNIQUES

At the initial stages when Reiki was practiced traditionally by touch, the recipient of the mediation used to be seated, lying down or standing. The treatment was conducted by placing the hand on the ailing part. Later Reiki developed into more sophisticated techniques which combine the practices of other alternative medicine ones including practices from different religions. As a result a number of advanced techniques are now practiced. In the literature available to me there is no criteria for classifying or categorizing the techniques of Reiki. However, for the purposes of this paper I am going to discuss them under ritual, spiritual and absentee treatments. All the advanced techniques require special skills and the practitioner or the individual who is going to practice it on his own must receive professional training.

RITUAL TECHNIQUES

1. Usui Technique

This technique is named after Miko Usui, a Japanese who attempted practicing and teaching a healing technique that was used by Jesus. His practice was first introduced in 1914. The technique depends mainly on the "laying on of hands"

> *"The story goes that Usui discovered ancient spiritual texts on energy healing techniques in a Tibetan Buddhist monastery. Usui then studied the texts extensively along with Sanskrit symbols. Shortly thereafter, Usui claimed he was hit by a beam of light, and had a spiritual experience. Usui claimed that through this experience he was spiritually given the method and symbols for the energy healing."(Advanced Reiki Inc.: http://www.reiki-healing.net/)*

Usui technique is the basic healing practice that strives to flow energy through touching the recipient and establishing the flow of energy that clears the pathway from blockage or negative energy. The traditional touch practice is clearly illustrated by Latorre, (2005):

> *During a traditional Reiki treatment, light touch is given on a fully clothed recipient who is either seated, lying down, or standing. A full treatment typically includes placing the hands in 12 positions on the head and on the front and back of the torso that correspond to the body's endocrine and lymph systems (Miles & True, 2003). Reiki can also be given in smaller increments if time is a factor and still be very effective (Fleming, 2003). As hands are placed on the body for*

3-5 min at each position, the energy flows according to the needs of the person receiving it (Miles, 2003)

2. Reiki Meditation With Second Degree Symbols

The rituals of this technique include position of body, environment, designation of a place, time for mediation and facing a wall. The recommended dose here is twice a day: once early in the morning before the day begins (which is the same time for the first daily prayer of Muslims) and another of the same duration before bed time (which is the same time for the last prayer of the day for Muslims)

In the mediation practice the requirement is:

> *"For the duration of your sitting, very gently and slightly turn your eyes up toward the spiritual eye. Meditation is basically a process of concentration, deepening and expansion. Another way to say it is that the consciousness and energy need to be withdrawn from the five senses, to become settled in the subtle centers along the spine, then directed toward the spiritual chakras, establishing oneself in the highest centers in the brain."*
> *(http://www.reikihelp.com/whatisreiki.html)*

SPIRITUAL TECHNIQUES

1. Reiki Prayer

This must be practiced in a form sitting as silent mediation and it is in all religions the surest way to "commune with the Divine."

> *Prayer can be a petition, asking for yourself; intercession, asking for another; confession, asking for forgiveness; lamentation, asking for fairness; adoration or devotion, expressing love, honor and praise for God; thanksgiving, a perpetual state of gratitude; invocation, calling forth the Divine Presence; and declaration, making a firm statement of truth. It can also be directed (specific) or nondirected (surrender).*

However, prayer is a profound and personal experience and there are endless ways in which to pray. (Pamir Kiciman (2004)

2. Reiki Personal Power Recovery (RPPR)

This technique, which is a step by step one, is facilitated by the use of a 'non-ordinary state of consciousness (NOSC)' that is also termed 'altered state of consciousness (ASC)'. It mainly depends on the expansion of consciousness and vision. Some conditions for this technique to be successful are stated in the following quote:

"This is a step by step technique that encompasses Reiki on the subtle bodies. It is a strong energy therapy and needs to be respected as such. The client's situation and response will modify each application. Work on the subtle bodies can be done within each Reiki session, whereas RPPR is an entire session on its own. You will develop an understanding that lets you know when this technique is appropriate." (Pamir Kiciman (2004))

The main concept of the technique is the management of the energy. However, this anonymous writer emphasises that energy is not the physical one that fuels the body for all its activity; it is rather the energy that including this one also comprises the '"quality and condition of vitality, the heart's harmony, the mind's focus and the soul's illumination." (*Advanced Reiki*)

In ritual techniques the objective is to achieve relaxation, reduce stress and hence develop harmony and balance by flowing energy freely (without blockages) and healthily through the body. The objective of RPPR is illustrated by the writer as follows:

"A personal power deficiency, seepage, or total unavailability is so common that healing could be essentially defined as the reclamation and proper distribution of personal energy and power. The soul is all-powerful. We are born with this power intact. What makes it a power is the soul's knowingness of its own nature: worthy, loved, joyful, beautiful, creative, limitless, a piece of God, a divine

design originated in truth and Light. However the karma game is that the soul continues to evolve and participates in the universal plan through physical incarnation. It has been doing this for eons. Each incarnation collects karma (literally action—every action has."
(Advanced Reiki)"

Finally, it is worth emphasising that this technique, and generally all Reiki techniques, cannot be practiced without the appropriate training. There are a number of websites on the Internet that offer training.

3-   Reiki as a Spiritual Practice

Drawing an analogy with business where 'best practices' lead to success, Pamir Kiciman (2005) asserts that 'spirituality' is the best practice of the human *'organization'*. The intangible and invisible spirituality represented by ki, i.e. life energy or vitality can be experienced. Based on this principle two meditation trainings are offered as the technique for this Reiki:

a- Breathing

It is the belief of the author that respiration is not limited to taking in oxygen and releasing carbon dioxide. For Reiki advocates breathing is a 'primary reflex' and in addition to the vital oxygen and carbon dioxide process, it also brings in fresh ki, representing life energy that is available in water, food and sunshine. It is strongly believed here that all the elements necessary for keeping human beings alive are useless without ki and even would not exist without it. (Pamir Kiciman, 2005)

Kiciman within this principle discussed above illustrates the role of ki as meditation in the following

> *"The meditations of Reiki are at the center of such a spiritual practice. These short and simple methods have a far-reaching effect and benefit based on meditative breathing, allowing the Ki of the Universe to replenish and refresh your personal Ki. As Ki is the subtle factor that **powers** all body parts and functions,*

*all-around health is directly related to the **quality** of Ki you have flowing throughout your body. The lifestyle choices you make and the multiple stresses of living in this technological, high-speed era usually diminish your Ki and even block its natural flow*

Ki is energy. Energy isn't limited to physical parts. Thoughts and emotions are a form of energy too. As the body is restored through meditative breathing, the incoming, pure Ki has a chance to clear out your emotions and thoughts, empowering you and creating balance, and bolstering you for whatever you'll be facing that day." (Pamir Kiciman 2005)

B- The *Hara*

Hara or belly resembles the physical centre gravity for the body. And spiritually "it's a seat of broad consciousness, a primordial connection to the Universe, a still- or one-point which exists and sustains you *before* and *after* the umbilical cord." (Pamir Kiciman 2005)

Kiciman further explains 'Hara' which he adopts from Buddhism:

"The goal of Reiki training and practice is to uncover this shining jewel, encrusted as it is with the accumulation of suffering, disease and delusion. Our human experience is limited, bound by time and space. Our spiritual experience is just the opposite; limitless, on a continuum and fully functional in the entire spectrum of Universal energy." (Pamir Kiciman 2005)

It is also Kiciman's believe that energy in our universe has two poles: Earth ki and Celestial ki. Within spiritual wisdom it is believed that by the union of these two energies exist all cosmos, planets, nature and its life forms, and human beings. He also emphasises that the energies mentioned here are not two different ones but rather "*two complementary poles of the same primordial energy. The whole range is spiritual, whether we split it in our perception as 'divine' and 'earthly.'*"

Then Kiciman further elaborates on the philosophy of spirituality – and I thin paraphrasing his words may not be accurate. Therefore his own words are quoted:

> "There are specific ways to embody, feel and integrate these energies in the course of Reiki training. Once proficient, a third state is born. This can be described as "oneness" or compassion. When the two poles are understood and realized by the practitioner, a blending occurs that creates unity, i.e., oneness. When you feel 'one' with yourself, others, your environment, nature and the cosmos, compassion arises because it leads to a deeper, visceral empathy with life. From this you progress to a level of higher enlightenment of **realizing** true unity consciousness.
>
> Earth Ki is a frequency of energy that helps the body heal and makes the mind strong. It helps to settle you in your center, creating a solid base to handle all manner of challenges, bringing order and power to your being and life.
>
> Celestial Ki is a subtler, more refined energy that helps to align you spiritually. It repairs spiritual disconnection and takes you to a higher consciousness. Your intuition becomes more and more reliable, and mental/emotional healing takes place." (Pamir Kiciman 2005)

Within spirituality Reiki practice, the objective is to create wholeness within oneself using the two frequencies which reunite the 'fragmentation and self-defeating patterns' into the "oneness" of self in relation t earth. This eventually makes life more meaningful, valuable and purposeful.

ABSENTEE TREATMENTS TECHNIQUES

It has been proved that Reiki can be practiced at a distance without having the practitioner's hand on the recipient. This was attempted on the belief that flow of energy is not limited by barriers and can travel across distances.

However, it is emphasised that greater level of concentration and deeper state of mental control is required.

The practitioners also recommend "objectifying" in which something at hand, at the end of the practitioner, is used to resemble recipient. This facilitates a direct connection with the remote recipient. Objectifying here is some kind of visualisation for the practitioner and requires deep concentration.

1. The Law of Correspondence with Absentee Treatments in First Degree

In this technique of sending Reiki at a distance, the simplest form is used. A photo or an object is used at the end of the practitioner to represent the recipient. Ere the practitioner uses the 'Law of Correspondence' or the 'Law of Similarity'. In explanation of the utilization of this law the following is quoted:

"This is the means for which you, the practitioner, tell the Universal Beings of Healing what you are intending to do, and how you are proposing to do that. Then they will help to hold your intent in place while you are the conduit of the energy of Reiki. Simply, the 'Law of Correspondence' states: "Each component within a system or thing retains its own characteristics and takes on the characteristics of the system or thing as a total sum of its parts". Hence, one human represents another or all other humans; or one thing represents any other thing. And the "Law of Similarity" simply states: "If a person, object, or condition bears any likeness or resemblance in color, shape, smell, action or sequence of events, it can be used for many psychic purposes as if it were the person, object, or condition itself, because of this likeness". Similar things have the same energy. So it is important to use either of these laws when doing any kind of distance treatments." (http://www.nyreiki.com/Advanced_Reiki_Training.htm)

This technique requires a lot of concentration and deep visualisation on the part of the practitioner who should establish in this way the energy connection to effect healing or establishing balance and harmony on the recipient at a distance.

CONCLUSIONS

In conclusion I would like to point out the following:

1. Within the limited space of a term paper (7 pages) it was not possible to cover all the literature and it was not possible to include a comprehensive list of the 'advanced Reiki techniques.
2. With a considerable degree of certainty I can say that Reiki practice is effective in healing and achieving harmony and balance for recipients
3. While it is possible for one to practice Reiki on himself, this cannot be successful without appropriate training.
4. Reiki can complement as alternative medicines and can also compliment modern science treatments.

REFERENCES

1. Honervogt, T. (1998). **Reiki: An ancient hands-on healing technique**. London: Henry Holt & Co.

2. Rebecca Debus **Reiki Healing For Balance And Harmony** – downloaded on 5 October from: http://www.alifehealing.com/reiki.html

3. Pat Cougar **A Sampling and Overview of Reiki and "Hands-On" Healing Research** downloaded from http://www.dpierce.com/reiki/reikiarticle.htm

4. Mary Ann Latorre (2005) **The Use of Reiki in Psychotherapy**. Journal: Perspectives in Psychiatric Care. Volume: 41. Issue

5. **Advanced Reiki Inc.**: http://www.reiki-healing.net

6. Miles, P. (2003). **Pamela Miles, Reiki vibrational healing—interview**. Alternative Therapies, 9(4), 74-83.

7. Miles, P., & True, G. (2003). **Reiki-review of biofield therapy history**. Alternative Therapies, 9(2), 62

8. (http://www.reikihelp.com/whatisreiki.html

9. Pamir Kiciman (2004) **Advanced Reiki Techniques:** http://www.reikihelp.com/whatisreiki.html

10. Pamir Kiciman (2005) **The Role of Spirituality in Complete Health** - http://www.reikihelp.com/whatisreiki.html

11. (http://www.nyreiki.com/Advanced_Reiki_Training.htm

CHAPTER III

The Reiki method of healing was developed by on the revelation by sensei Usui Mikao and the body's energy system to improve the quality of life. Reiki is used in self care and the care of others, also care in hospitals and care centers as well. The type of Reiki that people practice today has been present for over 100 years.

THE FOUNDER OF REIKI

The history of Reiki begins with its founder Dr. sensei Mikao Usui. Mikao Usui was born to a wealthy Buddist family in 1865. Dr. Usui's family was able to give their son a well rounded education for that time. Dr. Usui studied in a Buddist temple and learned martial arts and swordsmanship.

He also learned Chi Qong and Kiko as well.

throughout his education Dr. Usui had a particular interest in medicine and healing. It was this interest that led him to seek out alternative measures.

It is not a specific religion but Reiki works on the energy chakras for healing or treatment.

Dr. Usui traveled a great deal in his life for the purpose of learning and healing. systems are of all types and professions use Reiki. Reporters, Secretary, Nurses, Doctors, Surgeons. Dr. Usui lived in a temple

SPIRITUAL AWKENING AND DEVELOPMENT OF REIKI

Sometime during his career at the temple Dr. Usui attended his own training rediscovery in a cave on Mount Karama. For 21 days Dr. Usui fasted, mediated, on events that would alter his life a great deal.

Ancient Sanskrit symbols became a very important way of communication, it is still studied today. Dr. Usui studied Sanskrit for many years. Out of this the ancient way of Usui Reiki was born.

After the spiritual birth on Mount Karama, Dr. Usui established a Reiki clinic for teaching and healing in Kyoto. The practice spread and Dr. Usui became known as the father of Reiki.

SPREAD OF REIKI TO THE WEST

Hawayo Takata was in Tokoyo in 1935. Mrs. Takata was very ill and in need of surgery, but she strongly felt through her instiant that she didn't need that surgery to be healed. After asking her doctor about alternative treatments. Reiki was the answer they came up with. Mrs. Takata never heard of Reiki before As time passed in a meeting with Dr. Hayashi, Mrs. Takata, Much of this happened before world war II.Usui and Takata are seen as the main founders of Reiki.

Before he died Dr; Hayashi Dr. Usui managed to pass on all of his knowlege to mrs. Takata. She then passed Reiki to the western world.

She attuned or taught 22 people Reiki in the beginning. Today people use the practices of Usui for many different things. The genius of Reiki is that people can use it to heal themselves and animals as well. Reiki Masters can offer Reiki can offer Reiki to others using light static touch using prayer is also offered but is not required. It is offered for distant Reiki Reiki is a spirtual energy that we all feel and we may not pray but all of us care for our fellow humans. Reiki is a method developed by Mikao Usui. Reiki means 'universial energy'. The session takes place when the client is fully clothed, lying down and in a peaceful environment. The practioner places their hands slightly over the client to release the negative energies.

Many sensations may be felt.

CHAPTER IV

Reiki is a Japanese technique for stress reduction also promoting relaxation and healing. It is administered by 'laying on of hands' and prayer.

Reiki is based on life force energy. If the life force energy is low or we feel stress, maybe sick our life force is low. Rei means God's wisdom or Higher Power and Ki means life force energy forming the term Reiki life force energy.

A treatment feels like a wonderful glowing radiance through and around the client. Reiki treats the entire body emotions, mind and spirit. They create a beneficial effect. Reiki also works in conjunction with all other medical treatments and therapy techniques to promote healing.

Reiki is amazingly simple to learn, the ability to use Reiki is not taught in the usual way but it is transferred to the student through a Reiki attunement class. This ability is passed on through Mastership class with the ability to tap into the 'life force energy'

Its use is not dependent on the intellectual capacity or spirt level of the person. Reiki has been taught for all people of many backgrounds.

While Reiki is spiritual in nature, it is not a religion or dogma. There is nothing you must believe Reiki comes from God or Higher Spirit. Many people find the experience with Reiki puts them in touch with the spirt of that person.

While Reiki is not a religion, it is still important to act and live in harmony with other people. Mikao Usui, the founder, the founder of natural healing recommended that all cultures get along.

Today people practice Reiki may use the methods that were put in place by Dr. Usui. Dr. Usui was the founder of Reiki and Dr. Takata brought Reiki to the Americas. Reiki is practiced by many people worldwide. The genius of Reiki The practitioner learns the way of Reiki and passses it down to other people. This is called lineage. Modern Reiki masters may offer Reiki healing with static touch and light pressure as a conduit to the higher power. Reiki hand positions heal many different ailments to the human body.

CHAPTER V

Benefits of Reiki

There are many wonderful benefits of Reiki. Reiki is a very simple process but produces profound benefits for both client and practitioner. The main purpose of a Reiki treatment is not only to promote a better physical body but also to better the mind and spirit as well. The great thing about Reiki is that one does not have to be ill or going through difficult times to feel a benefit.

Some come to Reiki to help with their energy and chakra levels. Managing the stress of daily life is essential for people. Others will come to develop themselves spiritually and experience a greater meaning of their own well-being. Many clients and want to stay the way of Reiki.

After a treatment most clients feel relaxed and centered. Many who come find that it balances the energy system of the body. Reiki may reduce stress, anxiety, anxiety, pain, and infertility, just to name a few.

the main activity and job of the human body are many

Modify the activity of enzymes that result in reactions throughout the body.

Building muscle following sickness or injury via the transportation of amino acids to the muscle tissue, which is required to repair muscular damage to increase size and strenth.

Manage synthes of lipids by uptake into fat cells, which are converted to triglycerides

BENEFITS OF REIKI

There are many wonderful benefits to Reiki treatments. Reiki is a very simple process but usually produces many profound effects in the body. The main purpose of a Reiki treatment is not only to promote good physical health but mind, body and soul as well. Reiki helps to promote balance and harmony. It is effective and non invasive healing energy that flows throughout the body and may be used on any individual. Reiki works directly on restoring balance and works directly on restoring energies for the issue being worked on. Balance means physical, emotional and mental.

Left and Right brain, masculine and feminine. This would label things positive and negative.

2.   Creates deep relaxation and stress relief

What many people enjoy about Reiki treatments is it allows them time for just being. Clients have reported feeling more clear afterwards, peaceful and more positive.

Reiki provides a space where you can be more aware of what is going on in your life. Learning and listening to your own body and making decisions that will benefit the individual. Being more present means that you see yourself in your body and do the best for your body.

3.   Dissolves Energy blocks and promotes balance between mind, body and spirit.

Regular reiki treatments can bring about a calmer state of being. An individual is better able to cope with everyday stress in life. The mental balances also improves learning, memory, and mental health.

Reiki is good for mental and emotional worries and can help mood swings, fear, frustration and anger. Reiki is good for personal relationships.

Reiki can open up your heart to love others, relationships at work, family, friends and others may grow as well

4.   Assists the body in cleansing itself from toxins and support the immune system.

People spend so much time in fight or flight situations.that it becomes a regular way of life. The human body is out of balance. Regular Reiki treatments helps to keep the body in balance.

Reiki reminds our bodies to shift from parasympathetic nervous system to self healing mode.

Rest and digestion does not mean to stop your healthy way of life. Reiki is simply a supplement. The more you are able to stay in this space without being stressed produces greater harmony.

5. Clears the mind and improves focus and feel centered and focused

Reiki can support the individual to stay centered in the present moment rather than getting caught up on the past and future

6. Aids in Sleep

The main goal of a Reiki session is physical and mental relaxation.

When the individual receives better sleep. They can produce better energy in the moment. Often clients will experience q deep relaxation during a Reiki treatment.

7. Accelerates The Bodys Ability To Heal To The Natural State.

Reiki healing quickly returns the body to the natural state. This means breathing, blood pressure improve. Breathing deeper and easier is one of the first things noticed by clients. When we breath better our minds settle, this is studied by science.

As resperation decreases your body into the parasymphathetic nervous system or PNS Your body was made to function in the rest phase.

8. looking in on a Reiki treatment might look like a sequence of hand placements but it is how they are used in succussion by the practitioner to treat the client.

On the physical level Reiki helps with headaches and the client has better focus. Arthitis, sciatica are a just a few ailments that may be treated. It also helps with fatigue, asthma, symptoms of menopause. Sleep will tend to be better.

9. You do not have to be a spiritual person to receive Reiki. For many Re8i does increase their spiritual belief. The development of the client also grows as well.

Reiki addresses the entire person. Reiki targets the person rather than the symptoms. Many profound results can be found. Often subtle shifts in energy are found. Guidance about what to do around difficult situations.

The client has the ability to look at life from a fresh prescriptive. The Client may be led in a total different direction guided from within.

10. Compliments Medical Teatments and Other Therapies

1.Reiki is a wonderful compliment to many treatments. It helps patients keep a peaceful state of mind. A good physical is also kept because of the good state of mind. When the client and practitioner are relaxed the treatment is increased to a higher vibration.

11. You Can Learn Reiki for Yourself

1. Many clients will learn Reiki from themselves by attending Reiki I course so they can increase their own energy. Some clients are drawn to Reiki for breathing or personal development. They may go all the way to Mastership.

CHAPTER VI

The Throat or Vishuddi Chakra

The throat or Vishuddi Chakra energizes the throat, thyroid gland, parathyroid, and lymphatic systems. The chakra is located at the center of the throat. A malfunction in this chakra may result in a goiter, sore throat, loss of voice is possible. The Vishuddi Chakra also influences the Sex Chakra and therefore maintaing balance in the Vishuddi Chakra is important for health.

HEART CHAKRA OR ANAHATA CHATA CHAKA

The heart Chakra or Anahata Chakra is located at the center of the chest. The manipura chakra has a strong influence on the heart chakrsa. It is located in the back, The manipuca chakra controls and energizes the spleen. The physical heart is energized at the back of the heart.

SOLAR PLEXUS CHAKRA

Among the 2 parts of the Solar plexus or Manipura Chakra, the front solar plexus is located against the ribs and Manipuri Chakra is located against the back. The Manipura Chakra energizes the pancreas, liver, diaphragm and stomach. This chakra is also responsible for the quality of blood for the health of the intestine, lungs, heart and appendix.

SPLEEN CHAKRA OR PRANA CHAKRA

The name is self explantory. The spleen chakra is responsible for the health of the spleen both front and back. The spleen purifies the blood cells and destroys worn out blood cells. This is why diet is so important in life.

BASIC CHAKRA OR MOOLADHARA CHAKRA

The Basic Chakra is also known as the Root Chakra. If the root is strong, the tree will also be strong. If this chakra is not strong then the person may have a weak chakra. A strong root chakra results in strong muscles, skrlton,

MENG MEIN CHAKRA

The meng mein chakra acts as the pumping station in the spine and facilitates the flow of energy upward in the Prana from the basic chakra.

This chakra controls blood pressure, energizes and the kidneys. The Meng Mein chakra controls the internal and urinary system. This chakra should be treated only by experienced pranic healers.

NAVEL CHAKRA

This chakra energizes the small intestine, large intestine abd appendix

A malfunctioning navel chakra may cause disorders such as giving birth, constipation. An activated navel chakra ensures vitality in the individual.

SEXUAL CHAKRA OR SWIDHISTANA CHAKRA

The Swadishtana Chakra is located on the pubis. The sexual organs and bladder are energized by the Swadhistanta Chakra. This Chakra is strongly influenced by the Ajna, Vishuddi and Moolardnara Chakras. A malfunction in this area of the body could effect the sexual organs or bladder internally.

CHAPTER VII

Benefits of Sexual Energy

1. KEEPS YOUR IMMUNE SYSTEM WORKING

People who are sexually active and physically active have fewer sick days.

People who are sexually active can defend against viruses, and other bodily intruders. Researchers at Wilkes University in Pennsylvania found that people who had sex once or twice weekly had higher levels of antibodies compared to students who had sex less often.

Some of the following are suggested life practices.

1. EAT RIGHT
2. STAY PHYSICALLY ACTIVE
3. GET ENOUGH SLEEP
4. KEEP UP WITH VACCINES
5. USE A CONDOM IF YOU DON'T KNOW THE STATUS OF YOUR PARTNER OR PARTNERS

2. BOOSTS YOUR LIBIDO

Longing for a more lively sexual life. Having sex will improve the libido. This was studied by Lauren Streicher, M.D. at Northwestern University

Feinberg School of Medicine where she is an OB/GYN.

Research shows that sex and physical activity can lower blood pressure.

Joseph Pinzone studied the effect and he is the CEO and medical director at Amai Wellness.

he says many studies have been done. One landmark study shows that sexual intercourse specifically not masterbation lowered systotolic blood pressures.

Sex is a great form of exercise. It will not replace other exercises but it counts for something. Sex uses about 5 calories per minute, four more than watching TV. It gives a person a one-two punch. It bumps your heart rate and uses various muscles.

5. LOWS HEART ATTACKS

A good sex life is good for your well being. and heart. Besides being a great way to raise your heart rste, sexual activity keeps estrogen and testostrone in balance. Being out of balance may cause osteoporosis in an individual. Having sex more often may help During one study, men who had sex twice a week were less likely to have a heart attack.

IMPROVES SLEEP

Nodding off is a great reason to sleep after love making. After orgasm prolactin is released which is responsible for the feelings of relaxation and sleepiness. After love making says Sheerie Ambardar M.D. from West Hollywood.

10. EASES STRESS

Being close to your partner may reduce stress and anxiety.
Armbardar says touching and hugging can release the body's feel good hormone. Sexual arousal releases a brain chemical that speeds up your pleasure system. Making love and intimacy can boost the self esteem as well. It's not just a prescription for a happy one but a healthy one.

7. LSSONS PAIN

Before reaching for an asrin, try an orgasm. Orgasm can block pain says] Barry Komisaruk PH.D. of Rutgeers University. Sex releases hormones that help the pain threshold.
Stimulation without orhasm can do the trick. Vaginal stimulation can block chronic back and leg pain. Many women report that genital self stimulation can reduce cramps.

8. MAY MAKE PROSTATE CANCER LESS LIKELY

Going for the gusto may help ward off prostate cancer.

Men who ejaculated at least 21 times a month.were less likely to develop prostate cancer.

Though it may help you don't need a sexual partner to reap the benefits. Sexual intercourse and masterbation are all part of the equation.

CHAPTER VIII

Holistic Nutrition

CHAPTER VIII

The philosophy of holistic nutrition are many. It cares for the physical, mental and chemical should they be on medications. Using the holistic approach is better for the human body. To be balanced both alkaline and acidic. That is to say it is better for us to physically and mentally be centered in both areas. Eating heart healthy is a lifetime struggle for many.

It is difficult to balance a healthy lifestyle and diet as well. It requires alot of focus and energy. wisdom to live in ths manner. Many naturopathic advocate a healthy diet, There is much confusion how an alkaline diet can be achieved. It is important to understand does not mean the blood alkaline is normal. The body is like a battery if we keep it more alkaline than acid it is a healthy way to live.

CHAPTER IX

CHAPTER IX

We do aim to the scope and clarify the differences in the professionals that people may seek out. There are many health coaches and health nutrition professionals and to carry on with a healthy life we must know the difference.

Health coaching which is governed by the NBHWC otherwise known as the National Board Health and Wellness Coaches. Holistic coaches gain knowledge via interview techniques about the eating habits and activity habits of the individual.

The philosophy of the Nuturtion professional are many fold. Many aspects come into play for example physical, mental, chemical, emotional and spiritual. Coaches mainly work one on one with the client to schedule a nutrition and exercise plan. Holistic Nutrition professionals work with professionals such as doctors and other exercise experts for better health.

The whole person is treated physical, social, emotional, psychological,.

Fully engaging the individual as they proceed in the recovery process is important. Check-ins on a regular basis are done. The goals are different with each person as they go through stages and improve. each person as everyone differs. Health is many -fold, it includes pyscial, nutrition which pretty much go hand in hand. That is too say the majority of people that eat well have a good active life as well. Psychology and .social psychology or dealing with others. Eating better and a more healthful exercise life can lead to a good spiritual life for the individual.

Our bodies are like cars, airplanes, or motorcycles. If we keep the motor running clean we are alright. If we allow our body to get dirty or messed up so will we. Many health professionals throughout our lives have said

'You are what you eat' We are what we eliminate. We need to take care of our bodies and our environment. I will explain more in the following chapter.

CHAPTER X

At the end of the last chapter I began to explain rhe difference between 'we are what we eat' and 'we are what we elimanate'

The standard american diet is extremely unhealthy for the general population. It is even harder for an athlete and athlete in training. The overload of sugars, processed food are too high for the amounts of animal fats, chemicals and addiditives and many other foods. A athlete or person with a highly aciditic body count will recover more slowly. They will also experience more fatigue than most people. This may impair sleep habits, exercise, eating. It's important that the individual, no matter where they live, who they are, what they do keep in condition. As with any stressor the activity will cause the cortisol levels to lower and the amounts of growth will decrease. This increases a loss of mass. To make a health correction the frusturated athlete trains harder and longer. Without a proper recovery healing will not take place. Without acidosis causes the kidney stones and loss of bone mass. Since the body is effected on a cellular level the production of free radicals will increase.

Many viruses thrive in the acidic body. Conversely an alkaline body is more healthy and one people should strive to keep. Many athletes eat proessed protein bars full of preservatives. Drinkinh, Surgery and sports drinks take a toll on the human body and are not healthy. Paying attention to the alkaline-acidic balance is something everyone must do.

Acid farming is unheathy in anyones' diet.especially for athletes it is not good much less the person who is just walking around. It is still important to keep good health for the internal organs of our body.

Your body depends upon the health of the cells. One needs to main proper pH levels. On the pH level the top level is seven, and any level is alkaline. The chemical process is the best way to show the pH level. Blood has a pH of 7.4nd a dip lower than 7.2 can cause danger in the health of the individual. To avoid death your body will fight disorders to maintain homeostasis. If it means stealing whatever it needs to live, it will do just this.

Printed in the United States
By Bookmasters